Games for Kids
on
Horseback

16 Ideas for Fun & Safe Horseplay

Gabriele Kärcher

Translated by
Emma Josephine Didier

TS

TRAFALGAR SQUARE
North Pomfret, Vermont

First published in 2014 by
Trafalgar Square Books
North Pomfret, Vermont 05053

Originally published in the German language as *Spiel und Spaß mit deinem Pferd* by Franckh-Kosmos Verlags-GmbH & Co. KG, Stuttgart

Copyright © 2012 Franckh-Kosmos Verlags-GmbH & Co. KG, Stuttgart
English translation © Trafalgar Square Books

Trafalgar Square Books encourages the use of approved safety helmets in all equestrian sports and activities.

ISBN: 978-1-57076-652-7

Library of Congress Control Number: 2014930958

All photos by Gabriele Kärcher with the exception of p. 23 bottom and p. 25 top by Horst Streitferdt, Stuttgart.

Cover design by RM Didier
Typefaces: Charter ITC by BT, Matrix Script

Printed in the United States of America

10 9 8 7 6 5 4 3 2 1

Contents

Hi There!

Isn't sitting on a horse the best thing in the world? Well, that's how we feel, too! But sometimes we need a break from our regular riding lessons, and that's why we've created a whole bunch of games on horseback that we'd like to share with you.

These games aren't just a ton of fun, they also strengthen our partnership with our ponies—we become a real "team" as we ride through thick and thin together!

Whether you ride English or Western, whether your horse is calm and quiet or rather spunky, there are games here for everyone. Try them out and see which ones are the most fun for you!

Yours,
Sophia and Krissy

Ball Games:
Throwing and Catching

Even simple ball games can be a challenge when you're playing on horseback. It's pretty tricky to watch the ball and keep your horse under control at the same time!

Sophia and Julia have very well-behaved ponies that calmly stand still while the girls play catch.

Off We Go!

Before you begin playing throwing and catching games, you should make sure your horse is not afraid of the **ball**. On the ground with the horse standing still, take the ball in your hands. Rub it gently against your horse—his shoulders and withers are a good place to start—then carefully throw it up in the air (not too high) and catch it again. If your horse remains calm, bounce the ball on the ground beside him. When you can drop the ball near the horse's feet and he doesn't startle, try rolling the ball along his crest, between his ears, and over his head. Once your horse is accustomed to the sight, sound, and motion of the ball and is not at all upset by it, the game can begin.

The First Round

Start with two players on the ground and a third on his or her horse. The two players on the ground should throw the ball back and forth to each other first, and then include the rider when they are sure the horse is comfortable with the ball flying through the air. The goal is to keep the ball moving from player to player without stopping and without dropping it! Once the game works well with three players, add a fourth player on the ground—as well as a second ball. It'll be more difficult to simultaneously keep an eye on both balls and the horse—who needs to stay still, despite the shifting of his rider's weight in the saddle.

Sophia pays careful attention when the ball is tossed to her. Fortunately, she can rely on her pony Dusty.

Tip

Let your horse get used to the ball on the ground first. Let him sniff the ball, rub the ball against his body, and bounce the ball up and down beside him until you can trust him to remain completely calm.

The game is getting more difficult! Katie, Hannah, Julia, and Sophia have formed a team of four and are trying to keep the two balls up in the air as long as possible.

3

An All-Time Favorite:
Badminton

The point of this game is to try to keep the birdie in the air as long as possible. That's the only rule, but it's a tough one, especially when you're on horseback! Two players, two horses, two rackets, and a birdie are all you need.

Aim Well

Playing badminton on horseback is much more difficult than playing it on the ground because you can't move around as easily. That means having good aim is much more important when you're hitting in order to give your partner a chance to reach the birdie.

During this game the birdie may hit your horse, or your racket may brush up against him. Therefore, it's crucial that you familiarize your horse with these objects—first from the ground, then from the saddle. Show your horse the racket and birdie, and touch him with them on his chest, head, and croup.

The horses, whether ridden English or Western, should be quiet and should not be bothered by the flying birdie or their rider twisting around in the saddle.

Limited Range

The length of each player's arm and racket limits the space he or she can reach, since players can't move their feet! This makes the game challenging, and the birdie will often fall to the ground. After Katie and Hannah have dismounted and remounted again countless times to retrieve a dropped birdie, they realize: When playing "equestrian badminton," having a **helper** on the ground to collect dropped birdies is a huge relief! But most of all, you need two well-behaved horses that stand still and won't be upset by swinging rackets, flying birdies, and their rider moving in all directions while in the saddle!

Badminton requires both hands to play, so the horse must be able to stand still without the rider holding on to the reins.

Musical Chairs

You are guaranteed to have fun when you play musical chairs on horseback! When the *music* starts, all the players ride around a circle of chairs. When the music stops, everyone must try to find a seat. Unfortunately, there is one less chair than there are players. The player who can't find a seat is "out." Another chair is removed each round, until the winner is sitting in the only chair remaining!

To prepare, practice riding in circles of different sizes at a walk and trot. This will make your horse more supple and willing, which is crucial for playing musical chairs.

Preparation and Practice

On foot, this game is known and loved—and riders love it even more when it becomes a lively race on horseback. However, the game only works with obedient, well-behaved horses that won't kick or bite each other.

This game is best with five to eight players, on horses of about the same size. The chairs should be set up in a *circle* facing outward. (Outdoor chairs without hinges or sharp edges are a good choice.) There should be a horse-sized space between chairs so the horses won't get in each other's way when they stop.

To get the horses comfortable with this game, everyone should take turns riding around the circle, dismounting quickly, and sitting down—alone. Then the whole **group** can calmly do a test run at a walk, and then, depending on how advanced the riders are, a **trot**. If this goes well and everyone has their horses under control, it's time to choose a **music master**, who will be in charge of starting and stopping the music so the game can begin.

Be careful! If you rush too much, you might tip your chair (with you in it!) right over. Luckily, Sophia has a very good pony, who keeps calm when his rider goes flying.

Let the Music Begin!

It's critical for everyone to ride at the same **pace and tempo**, so the distances between horses stay equal and gaps are not created. After the riders have circled the chairs a few times, the music master must suddenly stop the music. The riders then halt, jump from their saddles, and try to find a seat on a **chair**. Players must not let go of their horses or tug on their reins. The player who doesn't find a seat is out, and one chair is removed from the game. As soon as the remaining players have mounted and reformed the circle, the music begins again. This pattern repeats until only two riders are left to battle for the last chair.

Tip

After every round, the players should switch directions.

*There can be only one winner! Whoever manages to sit down **first** on the last chair wins—even if two people can fit.*

7

Bucket Brigade!

"Water play" is always a blast, especially on a hot summer day! Here's a game that tests your agility and control: The goal is not to spill any water as you transfer it from one bucket to another. To do so, you need a steady hand and a well-trained pony that won't be startled if he gets an unexpected shower.

To play, set up two **barrels** in the arena or field, 3 feet (1 m) apart. A small bucket is placed on each barrel—one is empty and the other is full of water. Sophia begins the game by guiding Dusty between the barrels and coming to a halt.

The bucket of water is on Sophia's right, so she puts both reins in her left hand and reaches for the bucket with her right. Carefully, she lifts the **bucket** and moves it to the other side—without spilling a drop! Then she has to pour the water into the empty bucket.

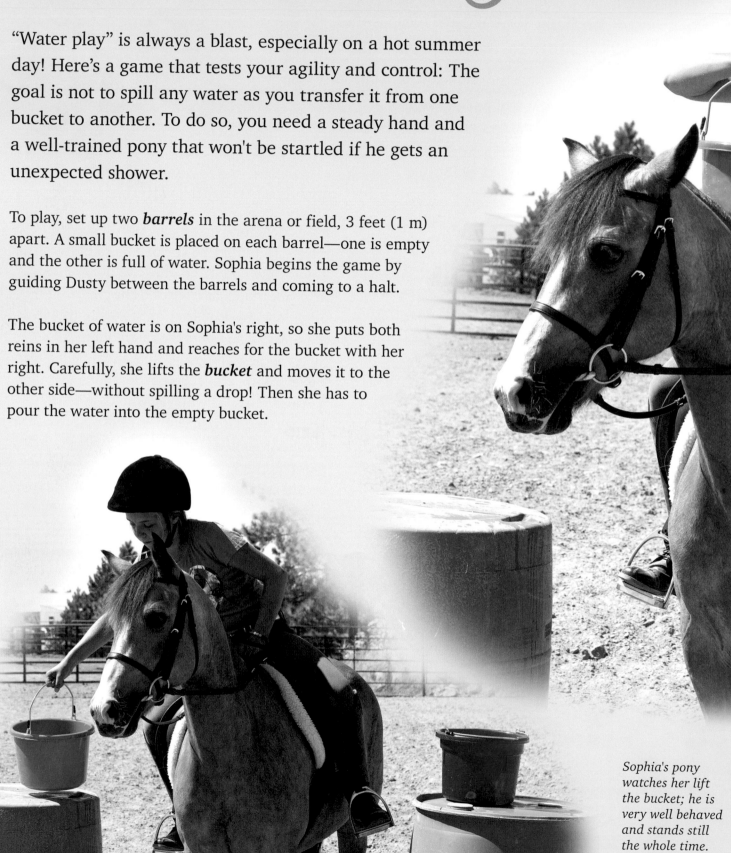

Sophia's pony watches her lift the bucket; he is very well behaved and stands still the whole time.

Gently supporting the bucket with the ***hand holding the reins***, she tilts it until the water flows into the empty bucket. Players with a horse that can be relied upon to stay still may be able to place the reins on the horse's neck and use both hands to pour. And remember not to spill the water! Why? Because at the end of the game, the amount of water in the second bucket (the one that was empty at first) is measured. The player with the most water in the second bucket wins.

Only for Water Lovers

If you want to make the game a bit easier, put less water in the first bucket, or replace the first bucket with a watering can. This makes it easier to tilt with one hand and pour precisely.

It's important to get your horse used to the sound and feel of water so he isn't surprised or startled by spills or pouring noises. Does your horse like the feel of a cool bath, or does he try to avoid water when it's time for you to wash him? Make sure he's comfortable with getting splashed before playing this game.

Some horses don't like standing between two barrels. To practice this part of the game, start with the barrels much further apart. Ride between them a few times and then stop in the middle, until your horse is comfortable with them. Then push the barrels a little closer together, and repeat the process.

Flowers and Potatoes

To add challenge, turn the **Bucket Brigade** (p. 8) into a more complicated game! Again, the horse stands between two barrels, but this time the rider's job is to fill a vase with water and then place a bouquet in the vase. The goal is to spill as little water as possible, and to get the bouquet into the vase without knocking over or dropping either one. (Dusty finds all this fascinating.)

Sophia rides her horse between the barrels. On top of one barrel is a **watering can** full of water, and a bucket holding a **bouquet of flowers**. On the other barrel is an empty **plastic bottle** (the "vase"). To keep the plastic bottle from falling over too easily, you can fill it part of the way with sand or gravel to help give it some weight.

Sophia leans to the right to pick up the watering can. Meanwhile, curious Dusty sniffs the "vase."

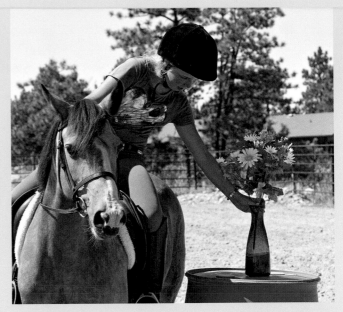

A fake flower bouquet with a single thick stem is the most practical option for this game.

Sophia pours water into the vase. Dusty helps her out by patiently standing still.

Sophia uses the watering can to pour water into the vase. Then she puts the watering can back and picks up the bouquet, and puts it in the vase. The narrower the neck of the vase, the harder it is to pour in the water—and slide in the bouquet.

Potato-and-Spoon Race

Another fun agility game is the potato-and-spoon race. Take a *large spoon* and balance a *potato* on it; hold on to the spoon with one hand and hold the reins in the other. See how far you can go without losing your potato—or who can cross the arena the fastest. To make it more difficult, go from a walk to a trot, or add a line of cones to weave through.

Katie carefully balances the potato on her spoon, and guides Daisy through the line of cones by shifting her weight, using her thighs, and neck-reining with her free hand.

11

Four Legs vs. Two

A race where one runner has twice as many legs—do you think that's fair? Horses are much faster than people, so isn't the winner already obvious? No way! Set up a special **obstacle course** where two-legged humans and their four-legged friends have an equal chance of winning. Speed isn't the only thing that counts—it's also about **agility**, concentration, and skill.

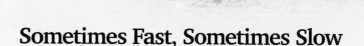

*You need to be able to control and **guide** your horse well to stand a chance against the runner.*

Sometimes Fast, Sometimes Slow

Two identical **obstacle courses** are set up side-by-side in the arena or field, separated by a row of **cones** or **poles**. The start line (which will also serve as a finish line) should be drawn about 30 feet (10 m) from the short side of the arena.

Another 30 feet (10 m) from the start line, the course begins with a line of poles set up in a "slalom" for racers to weave through. Often, the runner has an advantage here, but Dusty is well trained and trots through the pole slalom flawlessly.

Right after the *slalom*, place a single ground pole. Both two-legged and four-legged runners must stop here, one or two legs respectively on either side of the pole, and stay here for three seconds. Finally, at the other end of the arena, runners must round a barrel—without knocking it over!

Katie and her horse appear to be tied with Hannah—but the winner will be the one who's made the fewest mistakes.

A Strong Finish!

The *home stretch* can be ridden at a *canter* from the barrel all the way back to the start line, past the first set of obstacles. But watch out! Around 15 feet (5 meters) from the finish line, there should be a final *jump*, less than 2 feet (60 cm) high.

Scoring: The player who crosses the finish line first isn't always the winner. For each mistake—knocking over a pole in the slalom; not stopping at the ground pole for a full three seconds; tipping over the barrel; or knocking down the final jump—three seconds are added to a runner's time. The winner has the best *overall* time.

13

Boot Race

This game is best suited for riders wearing **cowboy boots**, or other types of proper riding footwear that can be pulled off and put back on easily. In this race, the players don't just have to ride fast—they also have to be able to take off and put on their boots quickly! Isabella, Laura, Krissy, and Daniela had a blast with their "boot race," and they want to show *you* how to play, too!

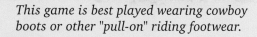

This game is best played wearing cowboy boots or other "pull-on" riding footwear.

Ready, Set, Go!

All you need for this game is an arena or field at least 66 feet by 131 feet (20 m by 40 m). There should be at least three players, but five or six is even better. Players need to line up along the short side of the arena with their horses' noses even. But they can't start yet! At the **signal**, the group must ride at a walk, **all together**, to the opposite side of the arena. There, everyone dismounts and takes off their right **boot**, making a pile at that end of the arena. Then the players mount up again, with one booted foot and one stocking foot, and ride at a trot back to the starting line, where they should turn around and line up a second time.

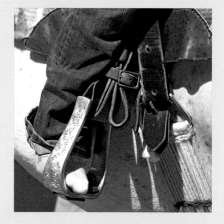

It feels strange to put your feet in the stirrups with nothing but socks on!

Tip

Riders in English apparel can play this game too, of course. It's just important for everyone to be wearing boots that are easy to remove—like "ropers" or slip-on paddock boots. High riding boots won't work because they're too hard to take off and put on by hand. Regardless of your chosen discipline, don't play this game while riding horses that have a tendency to kick or bite. When players are busy putting their boots on, the horses have to stand very close to one another, so it's important for them to get along.

Speed is good in a race, but if your horse is going too fast, it can be difficult to stop at the right spot.

Now the starting signal can be given again, and this time the horses are off! The players must ride as fast as they can to the pile of boots at the other end of the arena. There they must slow to a stop and dismount. Each player has to fish his or her own boot out of the pile— while remaining in control of the horse. If your horse pulls away, you lose! Everyone puts their boots on as quickly as possible, and then it's time to head back to the start line, as fast as you can.

Rushing too much won't help you, if your hurry disturbs your horse! You can only win if you hold your horse calmly while retrieving your boot.

Sit-a-Buck and Breakaway

In this "dollar-bill race," you must be able to sit on your horse as though glued in place, even without a saddle. If your *seat* lifts off the horse's back even a quarter of an inch, you'll lose your dollar—and the game! The key is to keep great contact.

Horses with smooth gaits make this game easier for their riders. Wendy is a good example—Hannah is practically glued to her back.

About half of the dollar bill is pinned underneath Hannah.

Wendy picks up a canter and Hannah's seat lifts for a moment—just long enough for the dollar bill to wiggle free.

Testing Your Seat

At a trot or a canter, it's easy to find yourself bumping up and down and getting thrown out of the saddle, unless you're in perfect sync with the horse's gait. This game encourages you to practice "gluing" your *seat* to the horse's back.

Players sit on their horses bareback, and each player needs a dollar bill (or a small piece of paper) to sit on. Each bill should be placed so about half of it is under the rider and the other half sticks out. Then everyone starts riding in a *circle*—first at a walk, which is easy. The challenge comes when you trot or canter! If your seat lifts off the horse's back for even a second, your dollar will fly away and you're out. The rider who keeps her or his dollar in place the longest is the winner—and knows she or he has a great seat!

Tip

Both horses must be ridden the same distance apart and at the same speed, whether at the walk, trot, or canter. To avoid biting or bucking, horses on a team together should be familiar with each other and get along well. Never use a "ribbon" that won't rip easily to play this game—you, your horse, or the other player or horse could get tangled up in it and trip or fall.

The "ribbon" Sophia and Krissy are holding is about 5 feet (1.5 m) long, and is made of thin paper that rips easily.

Breakaway

In this game, two riders have to complete an obstacle course *together*. It's important to maintain a constant speed and always keep the same distance between your horse and your partner's. Each player holds one end of a "*ribbon*," which should be made of material that tears easily—for example, crêpe paper. If the ribbon rips or either rider lets go of it, that team is out. First, they ride once around the arena at a walk, and then at a trot. Obstacles can be added: For example, a barrel can be placed at one end of the arena for a team to ride around at a trot. The pony on the outside of the pair will have to speed up a little and the pony on the inside will have to slow down in order to keep the ribbon from tearing. *Ground poles* that must be crossed as a team make another good obstacle to add to your course.

Both riders must be able to manage their reins one-handed, since they need a hand free to hold their end of the ribbon.

17

Wild-and-Crazy
Obstacle Course

Jumping, sidepassing, serpentines—these are the kinds of exercises you're used to in your regular riding lessons. Now this fun-filled obstacle course introduces a whole new set of activities to the players. The idea is simple: The players must complete a variety of "wild-and-crazy" tasks, and whoever takes the least time to do them is the winner. But it doesn't help to rush— each *mistake* will add extra seconds to your final time as a penalty!

1. Pole Salad

A bunch of ground poles in a disorderly pile make up the first obstacle. Let the reins hang loosely as you get close so your horse can get a good look at the mess he has to cross! Lightly touching or bumping the poles is allowed—but if any of them move, that's five *penalty seconds*.

Start

2. Putting on a Sweatshirt

Sophia rides to the next obstacle: a hooded sweatshirt on a hanger. The task is to put on the sweatshirt while sitting in the saddle, with the horse at a halt the whole time. If you know your horse is calm and will stand still, you can drop the reins—Sophia prefers to hold on to them and do her best not to bother Dusty. If you can't manage to put the sweatshirt on, or your horse starts moving instead of holding still, that's five penalty seconds!

3. Balloon Jump

Jumping is Dusty's favorite thing! The **balloons** are what make this jump difficult, waving and wiggling and moving in the wind. But Dusty stays focused, clearing the jump easily. If your horse refuses to jump, or knocks down the rail, that's five penalty seconds.

4. Boa and Scarf

A feather boa and sparkly scarf on a hanger make up the next obstacle. The feather boa goes around Sophia's neck; the scarf goes around her horse's! If the scarf or boa aren't properly tied and fall off, or if the horse doesn't stand still while you're putting them on, that's five penalty seconds.

Tip

Be careful when trying creative challenges like these. Horses instinctively run from danger, and are often afraid of new objects. Before you play a game like this with others, practice each obstacle by yourself. This way, you can get your horse used to the items involved. If your horse is really nervous, dismount and get him used to the new objects from the ground.

Finish

The activities that Sophia has shown you here are just a few examples. You can add all kinds of obstacles to your course: dismounting, running once around your horse, and getting on again; asking the horse to back up for several steps; or removing the bridle and bit and putting them back on. Let your *imagination* run free!

Barrels and Poles

"Barrel racing" and "pole bending" are popular rodeo and gymkhana events. In both, *speed* and *maneuverability* play major roles. In the first, you have to ride around three barrels in a specific pattern, and in the second, you have to weave your way through a line of poles. Speed is important, but you don't want to knock the barrels or poles over! If you can't slow your horse down in time to make a sharp turn, you don't stand a chance.

Krissy is a true master of barrel racing. She and her horse Bunny race around the barrels so fast her opponents can barely keep up. The fastest time wins, but Krissy rides carefully, too, slowing Bunny at just the right moment to get them safely around the barrels. After all, if they knock any of the barrels over, that's five penalty seconds.

With Speed and Skill

The three barrels are set up in a *triangle*. Krissy starts and heads straight for the first barrel, which is positioned on the right side of the arena with enough space between the barrel and the fence for her to circle it with a right turn. The second barrel is directly across from the first, on the left side of the arena. Krissy and Bunny circle this barrel with a left

turn. The third barrel is at the end of the arena, in the middle, and is also circled with a left turn. Pay attention: With every turn, the horse should cross back over his own path. Finally, horse and rider gallop from the last barrel to the finish line, where the clock is stopped.

The tighter the turn, the less time it will take. But you don't want to risk pushing the barrel over with the stirrup. If you do, penalty seconds will get added to your time!

Barrel racing and pole bending are fun for English riders, too.

Pole Bending

For this activity, the poles should be set up about 25 feet (7 m) apart. Krissy first rides past the line of poles, all the way to the end. Then she turns Bunny around and rides back, this time weaving through the poles as tightly as she can without touching them, in a *zigzag* pattern. When she reaches the last pole, she makes a sharp turn all the way **around** it and then weaves her way back through the poles. Then she and Bunny "head for home," galloping past the poles and all the way to the *finish line*.

Horse and rider must trust each other.

Tip

Krissy can gallop around the barrels and poles, but this took a lot of practice. To get your horse used to these games, try them first at a walk, and then at a trot. When a group of players is competing, set a required gait for each round so that everyone has an equal chance.

21

Stay Cool!

This game doesn't depend on speed or jumping skill, only your horse's nerve and ability to "stay cool." This is more of a test than a game, but it's still a fun exercise, and good preparation for other games and *special events*, like shows and trail rides.

Sophia guides her pony to the tarp and lets him get used to it.

Composure Can Be Learned

If you've ever gone on a trail ride, you know you're happiest when your horse doesn't follow his *flight instinct* every time a car passes by, a bird takes off, or you need to cross a stream. *Composure* is made up of *character*, *training,* and *trust*. Some horses are calm by nature; others need practice and training so they can learn to "stay cool." No matter what, a horse that trusts his rider and knows how to respond to a rider's signals will feel less vulnerable in new or frightening situations.

The "composure test" is made up of several different exercises that simulate situations you might run into at shows or on the trail. Sophia and Katie will show you a few activities that you can easily try in your own backyard. First, the girls spread out a *plastic tarp* on

It's important to let the horse take his time. Katie doesn't try to ride across the tarp until Daisy is totally calm.

Soon, Daisy's willing to carry Katie over the rustling tarp without hesitation.

the ground. Each player leads his or her horse across the tarp. Every time a horse sets foot on the tarp, it will rustle, which really scares some horses. This exercise prepares horses to cross unfamiliar surfaces or walk through water. Sophia guides her pony to the tarp and gives him time to inspect it. When he's not afraid of standing next to it anymore, she leads him slowly across it. Katie demonstrates the same exercise from Daisy's back. When a horse makes it all the way across the tarp, he deserves lots of pats and praise!

This pony trusts his rider, Sophia, and isn't fazed by the colorful balloons.

Balloons and "Noise Bag"

The point of this set of exercises is to get the horse used to objects that suddenly fly up out of nowhere! Have a friend hide in the arena, equipped with a few balloons that can be thrown into the air as you lead or ride your horse past. Sophia's pony remains calm. He trusts Sophia, and knows that the balloons aren't a threat if Sophia is so calm around them. You can also try having your helper open an **umbrella** in front of the horse.

The next exercise is to ride the horse past a rattling **"noise bag,"** which is a bag filled with empty cans and makes an impressive racket when shaken. It's also good to try some less frightening **obedience tests**—having horse and rider cross a square of ground poles, for example, or back up several steps. In every case, things should go smoothly, and horse and rider should demonstrate their trust in each other.

Horses are herd animals that tend to flee. If a horse's "herd member"— his rider—can make him feel safe, they'll stick together through thick and thin.

Scavenger Hunt

Up until now, all the games Katie and her friends have shown you have been played in a fenced-in field or in the arena. However, many games can be played out on the trail, or outside the usual riding areas at your home or schooling barn—including the ever-popular scavenger hunt. Not just a game of skill but also of agility and **knowledge**, this can be played individually or in teams.

Before you get started, mark the area of play. If there's a fork in the road or trail, you can use chalk to draw arrows on trees, rocks, or the ground, so the players know which way to go. Along the way, several **stations** are marked where various challenges await the players. This time, Hannah is the "game master," and came up with the following **questions** that have to be answered at each station: "What do you call a brown horse with black 'points' (legs, nose, mane, and tail)?" and "Where does the Fjord horse come from?" and "What do you call a mild, single-jointed bit?"

The Answer Lets You Pass

At other stations, players can earn points by completing various riding exercises, such as backing up a specific number of steps, or dismounting and remounting using a tree stump—which is only possible if your horse is calm.

Questions can be about horses—or about movies, music, or even math problems. Players need to be ready for anything!

Hannah is "game master," but also a station "judge." She writes down each player's answers and keeps a tally of points toward the final score.

Players can be asked to collect a certain number of things from the area of play—pine cones, for example, or the leaves of a particular kind of tree. Guessing games are also fun to incorporate into the scavenger hunt. Hannah has a big glass jar full of horse treats—she counted them earlier, before the game started. The players have to guess how many treats are in the jar, and the closer they are to the actual number, the more *points* they get. The treats then go to the horses to reward them when they've finished the scavenger hunt. *Judges* are posted at each station to award points. When coming up with activities to include, let your imagination run free!

One or more pieces of paper with questions are hung up on trees along the path. Players receive points for every correct answer.

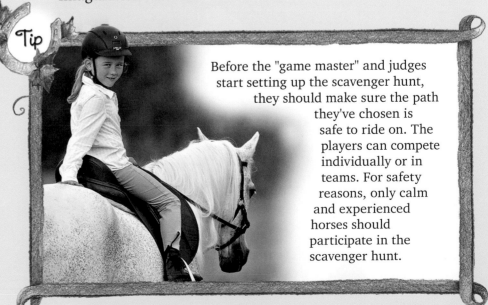

Tip

Before the "game master" and judges start setting up the scavenger hunt, they should make sure the path they've chosen is safe to ride on. The players can compete individually or in teams. For safety reasons, only calm and experienced horses should participate in the scavenger hunt.

25

Team Races

Games on horseback are all about having fun, trying new things, and participating. The popular gymkhana and other "mounted game" events were developed from playful at-home exercises into serious tournament sports. Players and horses have to be well trained to win **ribbons** or **trophies**.

Speed, Skill, and Imagination

Some of the games we've discussed are played individually or in pairs, but "mounted games" are played in teams. Each team is made up of five riders, four of whom compete at a time—the four who are best suited to the individual event. These four ride their event one by one. For example, pole bending (see p. 21): The timer starts as soon as the first rider crosses the start

In the "box race," each player must pick up a box from one platform and set it down on another before racing back to the finish line.

Small, nimble horses and ponies have an advantage in "mounted games" because the turns that need to be made are often quite tight.

line (which doubles as the finish line). Horse and rider weave through the poles both ways, and as soon as they've reached the **finish line** again, the second player starts. Only when the nose of the fourth horse crosses the finish line is the timer stopped, and this time is the first team's score. Then it's the **next team's** turn.

The games are all different, but all are fast-paced. Speed is just as important as being able to stop and turn precisely.

Goodbye!

Hopefully you already have plenty of ideas for how you can add to or alter the games we've suggested in this book. Every one of us has a favorite game, and even the horses like some games better than others. But that's also what makes these games exciting: There's never a horse that's the best at everything. Sometimes a calm, careful horse will have the advantage, and sometimes a speedy, spirited horse will.

We had to practice many of the games before we could really play them, and so we got to see how much horses and riders can learn from them. Games aren't just for having fun—they will also help you improve greatly as a rider.

Remember, safety is very important. The horses will often come very close to one another during these games, so it's important they don't bite or buck. But if you and your horse are prepared, you'll have just as much fun as we did!

Yours,

Thank You!

Without the help of our riders and horses, we would not have been able to present our games so clearly. We are very grateful to Katie, Sophia, Hannah, Krissy, Julia, Laura, Isabella, and Theresa. Thank you, you rode terrifically! Of course, we also want to thank their horses and ponies Daisy, Dusty, Wendy, Willy, Bunny, and Mirage. Our thanks goes to Linda, Robert, and Madeline Auch, as well, for letting us use their private ranch for practice and photo shoots, as well as helping tremendously with the photography.

Other great horse books for kids:

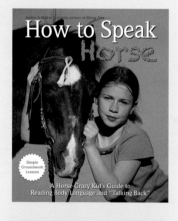

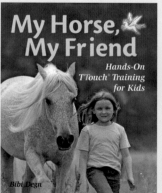